SH*T

JOE ROGAN

SAYS

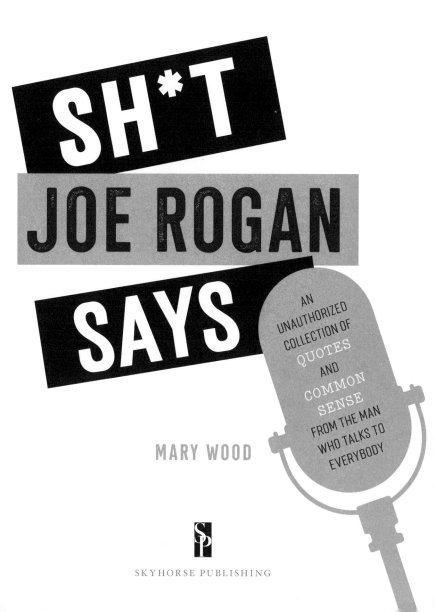

SH*T

JOE ROGAN

SAYS

AN
UNAUTHORIZED
COLLECTION OF
QUOTES
AND
COMMON
SENSE
FROM THE MAN
WHO TALKS TO
EVERYBODY

MARY WOOD

SKYHORSE PUBLISHING

CONTENTS

INTRODUCTION

Love him or hate him,
Joe Rogan has a lot to say.

His stratospheric trajectory to the number one podcast in the country, and one of the most popular in the world, has been fueled by his strong work ethic and love of a good challenge. His years in the martial arts, particularly karate, tae kwon do, kickboxing, and Brazilian jujitsu, taught him rigorous discipline and precise timing. And his years as a stand-up comic, Ultimate Fighting Championship commentator, and host of the reality show *Fear Factor* developed his chops for hilarious, off-the-cuff observations.

Most of all, Rogan is motivated by the meaningful, wide-ranging, and unscripted conversations he has with people from all walks of life, and he finds something to deeply admire in every single guest on his show. His tell-it-like-he-sees-it attitude has garnered both avid fans and ardent critics.

No matter what people think of him, he will never be hindered by the naysayers or political correctness—or polite language. Rogan drops f-bombs like there's no delay system or censorship on the radio—and for him, there isn't. Signing an exclusive multiyear deal with Spotify for $100 million allows him to say whatever he pleases, however he pleases. If anything, he'll never be accused of pandering to his audience or watering down his language.

SH*T JOE ROGAN SAYS is a collection of Rogan's take on everything from human beings' hunter-gatherer beginnings to the future of artificial intelligence. Along the way, he muses about life, comedy, happiness, free speech, politics, and his experiences with mind-altering drugs. Joe Rogan is an unconventional—and blisteringly funny—voice of our times.

PHILOSOPHICAL
MUSINGS

If you ever start taking things

TOO SERIOUSLY,

just remember that we are talking
monkeys on an organic spaceship
flying through the universe.

—Reddit post
August 17, 2015

THE WEIRDNESS NEVER ENDS, IT JUST CHANGES FORMS.

—Instagram post
March 19, 2020

ONE OF THE MOST DIFFICULT THINGS FOR PEOPLE TO DO IS TO CHANGE THE WAY THEY APPROACH REALITY ITSELF.

—*The Joe Rogan Experience*
June 24, 2019

Everyone is special
to someone or something.
We're all the same. We're
all a part of this weird,
crazy, gigantic organism
that's the human race.

—*The Joe Rogan Experience*
January 16, 2019

WE'RE CONNECTED IN SOME STRANGE WAY THAT WE DON'T TOTALLY UNDERSTAND.

—YouTube video
November 7, 2017

IN ALL MY TRAVELINGS,
ALL MY LIFE ADVENTURES,
I HAVE TO SAY I STILL
DON'T KNOW WHAT
LIFE IS, ABSOLUTELY
NO CLUE, AND IT IS
A SUBJECT THAT
IS CONSTANTLY
ON MY MIND.

—*Joe Rogan: How to Win the Game of Life*, by Alex Karadzin, 2021

YOU'RE JUST
part of the soup
OF THE UNIVERSE,
so just try to
ENJOY WHAT'S
good about it.

—Interview with Steph Daniels
May 15, 2014

We learn the building blocks of mathematics, the fundamentals of language, the facts of history—but we never learn how to manage our minds. We never learn how to live by a code and to surround yourself with like-minded people and to inspire and encourage each other.

—*Caveman Circus*
March 28, 2013

PEOPLE ARE SCARED, MAN

THEY'RE SCARED OF THE VOID.

—*The Joe Rogan Experience*
April 30, 2012

REALITY REALLY IS A THEATER.

There's no other
way to describe it.
It's all so nonsensical,
ridiculous, and chaotic.

—*Joe Rogan: A Biography*, by Nicholas Voth, 2020

I BELIEVE THAT IF WE DON'T BLOW OURSELVES UP, OR POISON OURSELVES WITH POLLUTION, OR GET WIPED OUT BY A SUPER-BUG OR AN ASTEROID IMPACT, WE'LL SLOWLY COME TO THE UNDERSTANDING THAT WE REALLY ARE JUST ONE SPECIES, AND THAT THE ONLY WAY TO TRULY BE HAPPY IS IF EVERYONE AROUND YOU IS HAPPY AS WELL.

—*Caveman Circus*
March 28, 2013

LIFE IS STRANGE.

YOU KEEP MOVING AND KEEP GROWING. BEFORE YOU KNOW IT, YOU LOOK BACK AND THINK, "WHAT WAS THAT?"

—Interview with Randy Cordova
December 9, 2014

"

LIKE BEES CREATING A BEEHIVE OR ANTS CREATING AN ANTHILL, *we're all moving along creating something and we're not sure what it is.*

—Interview with *Brightest Young Things*
   September 29, 2011

[YOU HAVE TO] RESPECT THE MECHANISM OF HAPPINESS AND FULFILLMENT AND *what you really need to do in order to feel satisfied in life.*

—YouTube video
June 19, 2021

> **THE HUMAN ORGANISM, THE ANIMAL THAT WE ARE, NEEDS CONSTANT STIMULATION BECAUSE IT EVOLVED TRYING TO FIND FOOD AND ESCAPE ENEMIES AND FIND SHELTER AND ESCAPE THE ELEMENTS.**

—YouTube video
June 19, 2021

YOU CAN TELL A LOT FROM

someone about how much attention they spend . . . pointing out other people's failures and how little time they spend reflecting on their own.

—YouTube video
April 14, 2021

The quicker
we all realize that
we've been taught how
to live life by people
that were operating on the
momentum of an ignorant
past, the quicker we can
move to a global ethic of
community that doesn't value
invented borders or the
monopolization of natural
resources, but rather the
goal of a happier, more
loving humanity.

—Reddit post
November 20, 2014

You are one
miniscule piece
of a never-ending
cycle. In fact,
you're not even
a piece. You're
just a holder
for billions and
billions of
other pieces.

—Interview with Steph Daniels
May 15, 2014

TALKING TO
EVERYBODY

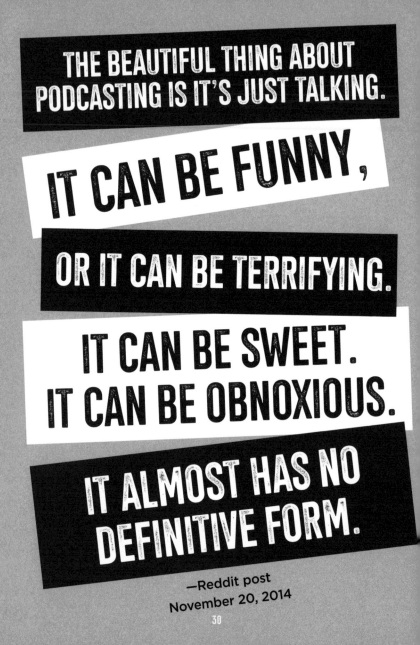

THE BEAUTIFUL THING ABOUT PODCASTING IS IT'S JUST TALKING.

IT CAN BE FUNNY,

OR IT CAN BE TERRIFYING.

IT CAN BE SWEET.
IT CAN BE OBNOXIOUS.

IT ALMOST HAS NO DEFINITIVE FORM.

—Reddit post
November 20, 2014

I'VE ALWAYS BEEN CURIOUS,
BUT I'VE LEARNED HOW TO BE
MORE EFFECTIVELY CURIOUS
AS I'VE GOTTEN OLDER.

—Interview with
Breaking Points
June 17, 2021

IT'S A STRANGE *responsibility* **TO HAVE THIS MANY** *viewers and listeners.* **IT'S NOTHING THAT** *I prepared for,* **AND IT'S NOTHING THAT** *I ever anticipated.*

—*LA Times*
January 30, 2022

WHAT THE
PODCAST SERVES
IS IT ALLOWS ME TO
HAVE VERY LONG
CONVERSATIONS
[WITH PEOPLE] THAT
I PROBABLY WOULD
NEVER HAVE THE
CHANCE TO SIT DOWN
AND TALK TO.

—Interview with *Brightest
Young Things*
October 16, 2014

There's no way
I can understand
what's going on in your
head other than you
telling me about it and
me trying to decipher it
and trying to put it into
words. . . . And I've tried
to look at life through
other people's eyes, and the
only way you get that is
through them talking.

—*The Joe Rogan Experience*
May 26, 2020

MY POINT OF DOING THIS *is always just to* CREATE INTERESTING *conversations,* AND ONES THAT *I hope people enjoy.* SO IF I PISS YOU OFF, *I'm sorry, and if you* ENJOYED THE PODCAST, *thank you.*

—*LA Times*
January 30, 2022

HAVING A PODCAST DEFINITELY FEEDS MY CURIOSITY, STIMULATES IT, AND IT ALSO ALLOWS ME TO HAVE MORE SUBJECT MATTER, MORE FOR STANDUP, MORE FUEL FOR MY MIND.

—Interview with *Brightest Young Things*
October 16, 2014

I'M NOT INTO ESCAPE. I DON'T WANT TO ESCAPE. I WANT TO DIG DEEP.

—*The Joe Rogan Experience*
May 26, 2020

> **Having the privilege of SITTING DOWN AND HAVING three-hour-long UNINTERRUPTED CONVERSATIONS with hundreds of brilliant PEOPLE IS AN AWESOME perspective enhancer.**
>
> —Reddit post
>   November 20, 2014

Anybody who sets out
TO BE A CRITIC IS A LOSER.
That is a fact.

—Interview with *The Daily Show with Jon Stewart*
August 7, 2001

DISCIPLINE AND
MOTIVATION

TO ME, THE MOST EXCITING
THING IS TO TRY TO GET
BETTER AT SOMETHING,
TO LEARN THINGS.
I MEAN, IT'S REALLY
EXCITING WHEN YOU
JUST HAVE INCREMENTAL
PROGRESS IN SOMETHING
THAT YOU'RE
COMPLETELY
NEW TO.

—*The Joe Rogan Experience*
   June 24, 2019

YOU HAVE TO BE
ABLE TO HAVE [AN]
HONEST ASSESSMENT
OF YOURSELF AND
THE ONLY WAY YOU
CAN DO THAT IS IF
YOU'RE TAKING
ACCOUNT OF
YOURSELF ALL
DAY LONG.

—YouTube video
March 3, 2018

Through difficult tasks you
learn an incredible amount

ABOUT YOURSELF.

Through the fire of competition
you get to understand the resistance
that you have inside your mind.
Doing the hard work you get to
understand the rewards of discipline.

—YouTube video
November 7, 2017

IF YOU DON'T TAKE CARE OF YOUR HEALTH, IT'S NOT JUST BAD FOR YOU. IT'S BAD FOR THE PEOPLE AROUND YOU.

—*Joe Rogan: How to Win the Game of Life*, by Alex Karadzin, 2021

Your mind
has to seek
discomfort.
It has to
seek out the
difficult tasks
and you have
to figure out
a way to make
your mind enjoy
those things.

—YouTube video
April 14, 2021

MY COMMITMENT
IS JUST TO DO
THE BEST JOB
THAT I CAN.

—Interview with *Breaking Points*
June 17, 2021

DISCOMFORT IS YOUR FRIEND. NOT BEING HAPPY AND CONTENT WITH CERTAIN SITUATIONS IN LIFE ARE MASSIVE MOTIVATORS AND THEY'RE AMAZING AT FACILITATING CHANGE.

—YouTube video
November 7, 2017

Every single person who has ever done anything worthwhile or exceptional or difficult or extraordinary . . . encounters difficulties. There is no easy road. Those difficult moments are what build your character.

—YouTube video
November 7, 2017

49

NO ONE SETS OUT TO MAKE THEIR LIFE'S WORK TO CRITIQUE OTHER PEOPLE'S CHANCES. THOSE PEOPLE ARE ALL PUSSIES, EVERY SINGLE ONE OF THEM.

—Interview with *The Daily Show with Jon Stewart*
August 7, 2001

THE ONLY WAY YOU
EVER GET WHERE YOU WANT TO
GO IS YOU HAVE TO TAKE A PATH
THAT IS DANGEROUS. MOST
PEOPLE WANT TO TAKE THE
SAFE PATH, AND THE SAFE
PATH LEAVES YOU STUCK
IN QUIET DESPERATION
ALMOST EVERY TIME.

—*The Joe Rogan
Experience*
May 15, 2019

CONSISTENCY [IS]
just showing up
WHEN YOU DON'T
want to show up,
FORCING YOURSELF
to do things you
DON'T WANT TO DO,
but then reaping
THE REWARDS.

—YouTube video
April 14, 2021

I am a grinder.
I get up every
morning and I grind.
People think you have
to have a vision board
to get started. I keep my
head down and grind and
when the time comes I
just decide if I want
to keep doing it.

—*Joe Rogan: How to Win
the Game of Life*, by
Alex Karadzin, 2021

EXCELLENCE
IN ANYTHING
INCREASES
YOUR POTENTIAL IN
EVERYTHING.

—Twitter post
December 27, 2009

HATERS ARE ALL FAILURES.

It's 100 percent across the board. No one who is truly brilliant at anything is a hater.

—*Joe Rogan: Podcasts, Pot, and Persistence,* by James Woolf, 2020

PEOPLE ARE SCARED OF FAILURE . . . BUT FAILURE IS ONE OF THE MOST IMPORTANT THINGS YOU COULD EVER HAVE AS FAR AS THE MOTIVATION TO DO THINGS DIFFERENTLY.

—YouTube video
  November 7, 2017

GREATNESS AND MADNESS

ARE NEXT DOOR NEIGHBORS
AND THEY OFTEN BORROW
EACH OTHER'S SUGAR.

—*Joe Rogan: A Biography*,
by Nicholas Voth, 2020

I think it's important
to have those jobs
that suck, man.
They cement your
foundation. . . .
But if you can get
through that. . . .
Guess what? You're
going to get up and
do things you
love easier.

—*The Joe Rogan Experience*
May 26, 2020

I AM THE LAZIEST DISCIPLINED PERSON I KNOW

—Joe Rogan: How to Win the Game
of Life, by Alex Karadzin, 2021

"

[You've] got to balance
DISCIPLINE AND ENTHUSIASM.
Discipline's critical.
YOU HAVE TO BE ABLE TO SHOW
up, but you also have
TO ENJOY THE SHIT OUT OF IT.

—*The Joe Rogan Experience*
  May 26, 2020

Your attitude has a **GIANT EFFECT NOT JUST** *on your life, but on* **OTHER PEOPLE'S LIVES** *around you.*

—*Joe Rogan: Podcasts, Pot, and Persistence*, by James Woolf, 2020

JUST FUCKING DO IT.

—Joe Rogan: How to Win the Game of Life, by Alex Karadzin, 2021

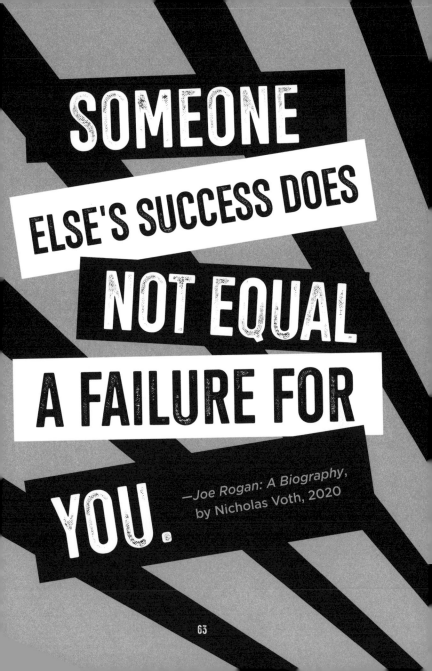

SOMEONE ELSE'S SUCCESS DOES NOT EQUAL A FAILURE FOR YOU.

—*Joe Rogan: A Biography,*
by Nicholas Voth, 2020

There's only one way TO GET GOOD AT ANYTHING; YOU SURROUND YOURSELF WITH *the bad motherfuckers* WHO ARE DOING EXACTLY WHAT YOU WANT TO DO AND *you force yourself to keep* UP AND INSPIRE EACH OTHER.

—*Joe Rogan: A Biography*, by Nicholas Voth, 2020

Don't let the world maintain your mind-set. YOU CHOOSE WHAT MIND-SET YOU ARE GOING TO MAINTAIN.

—YouTube video
March 3, 2018

I THINK SOMETIMES *people are scared* **OF IMPROVEMENT BECAUSE THEY'RE** *scared of failure.* **SO IF THEY CAN JUST KIND OF SLIDE INTO** *the same bullshit* **EVERY DAY, IT MAKES THEM FEEL LESS UNEASY.**

—*The Joe Rogan Experience*
May 26, 2020

THERE'S A LOT OF PEOPLE THAT ARE BULLSHITTING ONLINE. THERE'S A LOT OF THESE MOTIVATIONAL SPEAKERS THAT HAVEN'T DONE SHIT.

—*The Joe Rogan Experience*
May 26, 2020

MARTIAL
ARTS

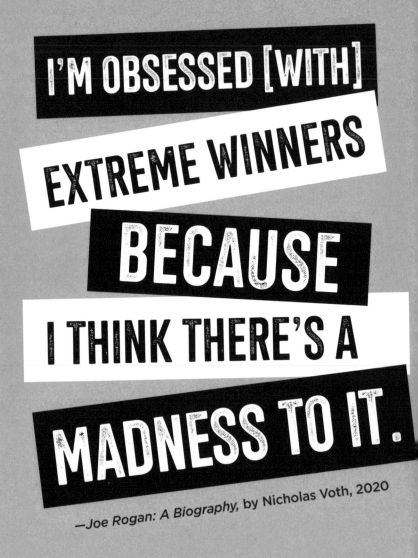

I'M OBSESSED [WITH] EXTREME WINNERS BECAUSE I THINK THERE'S A MADNESS TO IT.

—Joe Rogan: A Biography, by Nicholas Voth, 2020

MARTIAL ARTS IS A VEHICLE FOR DEVELOPING YOUR HUMAN POTENTIAL.

—*Joe Rogan: A Biography*,
by Nicholas Voth, 2020

[Jujitsu is] essentially like a language with your body. Like you're having an argument with someone with some sort of a physical language. And it's really complex and the more access to vocabulary and the sharper your words are, the more you'll succeed in these ventures.

—*The Joe Rogan Experience*
May 7, 2020

THERE'S A CONFIDENCE *and a mental toughness* **THAT COMES FROM THE** *very highest level* **OF COMPETITION,** *whatever the sport is.*

—*Joe Rogan: A Biography,*
by Nicholas Voth, 2020

ONCE YOU UNDERSTAND
WHAT EXCELLENCE IS
ALL ABOUT, WHETHER
IT'S IN PAINTING, OR
CARPENTRY OR MARTIAL
ARTS, THEN YOU SEE
HOW THAT EXCELLENCE
MANIFESTS ITSELF
IN ANY DISCIPLINE.

—Interview with Steph Daniels,
   May 15, 2014

I SEE MARTIAL ARTS AS MOVING FORMS OF MEDITATION. WHEN YOU'RE SPARRING OR DRILLING TECHNIQUES, YOU CAN'T THINK OF ANYTHING ELSE.

—*Joe Rogan: Podcasts, Pot, and Persistence,* by James Woolf, 2020

Martial arts was the
first thing that gave me

CONFIDENCE

that I wasn't going
to be a loser.

—*Joe Rogan: Podcasts, Pot, and Persistence*, by James Woolf, 2020

THERE'S A DIRECT CORRELATION BETWEEN POSITIVE ENERGY AND POSITIVE RESULTS IN THE PHYSICAL FORM.

—*Joe Rogan: Podcasts, Pot, and Persistence*, by James Woolf, 2020

BY PUTTING YOURSELF IN THAT INTENSE FORM OF STRESS, IT MAKES REGULAR LIFE MORE PEACEFUL.

—*Joe Rogan: A Biography,*
by Nicholas Voth, 2020

Martial arts gave me not just confidence, but also a different perspective of myself and what I was capable of. I knew that I could do something I was terrified of and that was difficult and that I could excel at it.

—*Joe Rogan: Podcasts, Pot, and Persistence,* by James Woolf, 2020

WORKOUTS AND THINGS YOU DON'T WANT TO DO KEEP YOU GROUNDED. THEY KEEP YOU ROOTED IN THE REALITY OF THE STRUGGLE.... ONCE I HAVE THAT, I CAN BE MORE APPRECIATIVE OF EVERYTHING I HAVE. I CAN BE A MORE LOVING HUSBAND, FATHER, FRIEND.

—*Joe Rogan: How to Win the Game of Life,*
   by Alex Karadzin, 2021

I TRULY BELIEVE
THAT IN ORDER TO BE
TRULY GREAT
AT SOMETHING YOU HAVE
TO GIVE IN TO A CERTAIN
AMOUNT OF MADNESS.

—*Joe Rogan: A Biography*,
by Nicholas Voth, 2020

LIVING IN THE
MODERN WORLD

SO INSTEAD OF INVESTING
your time in a passion,
YOU'VE SOLD YOUR LIFE
to work for an
UNCARING MACHINE THAT
doesn't understand you.
THAT'S THE PROBLEM
with our society.
AND WHAT'S THE REWARD?
Go home and get a big TV.

—YouTube video
February 19, 2015

One of the horrible things about kids growing up today is that they do have all this stuff out there on social media forever. They can be judged horribly by something they did when they were thirteen.

—*The Joe Rogan Experience*
October 23, 2019

> **ARTIFICIAL INTELLIGENCE AND THE RISE OF A SENTIENT, COMPLETELY MANUFACTURED, SUPER-INTELLIGENT LIFE FORM ARE A HUGE THREAT TO THE HUMAN RACE, BUT I THINK HUMANS MERGING WITH TECHNOLOGY AND BECOMING CYBORGS MIGHT JUST HAPPEN BEFORE THAT.**

—Instagram post
November 13, 2021

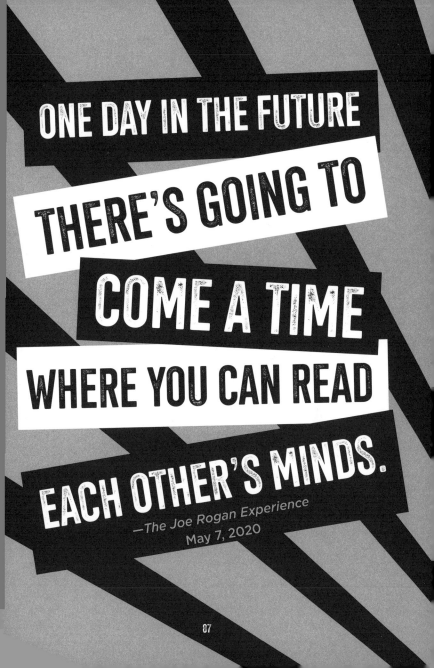

ONE DAY IN THE FUTURE THERE'S GOING TO COME A TIME WHERE YOU CAN READ EACH OTHER'S MINDS.

—*The Joe Rogan Experience*
May 7, 2020

[SOCIAL MEDIA] IS SUCH A WEIRD WAY TO DISPLAY YOUR LIFE BECAUSE, YOU KNOW, YOU'RE DISPLAYING THE BEST ASPECTS OF YOUR LIFE IN SOME SORT OF GLASS CASE. IT'S AN UNREALISTIC VERSION OF YOUR LIFE THAT YOU CULTIVATE.

—*The Joe Rogan Experience*
June 24, 2019

WE HAVE BEEN FED THIS LINE OF HORSESHIT THAT YOU'RE SUPPOSED TO SEEK COMFORT, AND I DON'T THINK YOU ARE. I THINK YOU'RE SUPPOSED TO SEEK LESSONS AND YOU'RE SUPPOSED TO SEEK DIFFICULT TASKS.

—YouTube video
June 19, 2021

IF WE CONTINUE TO LOSE EMOTIONAL INTELLIGENCE, IT WILL MAKE IT A LOT EASIER TO LOSE EMOTIONS ALTOGETHER.

—Instagram post
November 13, 2021

WE STILL CONCENTRATE ON NEGATIVE COMMENTS,

negative stories, these negative things carry more weight because we have a natural inclination to keep an eye out for danger. It's like our human reward system has been hijacked.

—*The Joe Rogan Experience*
May 26, 2020

WE'RE CONSTANTLY *reevaluating the* **POTENTIAL FOR LIFE.** . . . *We're finding life* **IN THE INCREDIBLY HARSH** *and dynamic conditions,* **SO WE'RE HAVING TO** *reevaluate our own ideas* **ON WHAT'S POSSIBLE** *on this planet alone.*

—*Joe Rogan: Podcasts, Pot, and Persistence,* by James Woolf, 2020

I THINK IT'S HARD TO SEE BECAUSE WE'RE IN THE MIDDLE OF IT, BUT I THINK HISTORY IS GOING TO STUDY US CAREFULLY, AND THERE'S GOING TO BE A LOT OF SCHOLARS STUNNED THAT OUR CIVILIZATION FELL APART SO QUICKLY.

—Instagram post
April 4, 2022

IT SEEMS LIKE OUR DATA BECAME A COMMODITY BEFORE WE UNDERSTOOD WHAT IT WAS. . . . AND ONCE EVERYONE'S ACCUSTOMED TO THIS SITUATION, IT'S VERY DIFFICULT TO PULL THE REINS BACK. IT'S VERY DIFFICULT TO TURN THAT HORSE AROUND.

—*The Joe Rogan Experience*
October 23, 2019

No matter how civilized we are and how much society has curbed violent behavior, human beings still have the same genes they had 10,000 years ago. Our bodies are designed to have a certain amount of physical stress and violence in them. We're designed to run from jaguars and fight to defend our territory.

—*Joe Rogan: A Biography*, by Nicholas Voth, 2020

FREEDOM OF
SPEECH

> ## IF I PAID ATTENTION TO ALL OF IT THEN I WOULDN'T BE ABLE TO DO ANY OF THE THINGS I WANT TO DO.
>
> —Interview with *Breaking Points*
> June 17, 2021

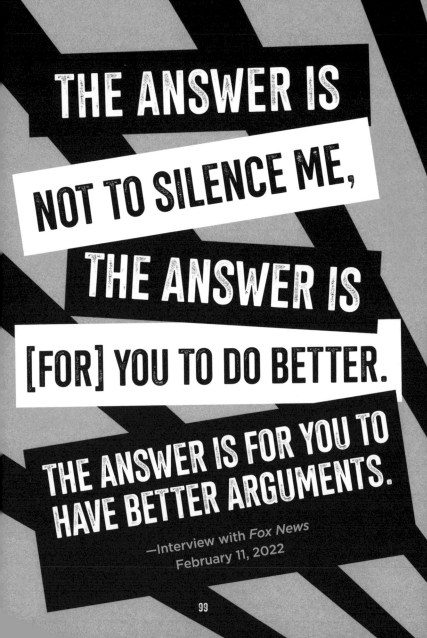

THE ANSWER IS NOT TO SILENCE ME, THE ANSWER IS [FOR] YOU TO DO BETTER. THE ANSWER IS FOR YOU TO HAVE BETTER ARGUMENTS.

—Interview with *Fox News*
February 11, 2022

WHEN SOMEONE *comes along* **AND EXPRESSES** *him or herself* **AS FREELY AS** *they think,* **PEOPLE FLOCK TO IT.** *they enjoy it.*

—*Joe Rogan: How to Win the Game of Life,* by Alex Karadzin, 2021

PEOPLE ON NETWORK TV DON'T HAVE ANYTHING REMOTELY SIMILAR TO THE KIND OF FREEDOM I ENJOY DOING THE PODCAST.

—Instagram post
October 15, 2021

THE THING ABOUT PODCASTS
IS YOU'RE PROFESSIONALLY
UNPROFESSIONAL. . . . IF YOU'RE
DOING IT WELL YOU'RE MAKING
THESE PEOPLE FEEL LIKE [THEY'RE]
JUST TALKING TO SOMEONE WHO
CARES. . . . THE ONLY WAY TO DO
THAT IS TO ACTUALLY CARE.

—Interview with *Breaking Points*
   June 17, 2021

IF YOU WANT MY ADVICE,

DON'T TAKE MY ADVICE.

—Daily Mail
February 10, 2022

WHEN YOU HAVE SOMETHING THAT CAN'T GET CANCELED, YOU CAN BE FREE.

—*Screen Rant*
May 27, 2020

THE PROBLEM THAT I HAVE WITH MISINFORMATION, ESPECIALLY TODAY, IS THAT MANY OF THE THINGS THAT WE THOUGHT OF AS MISINFORMATION JUST A SHORT WHILE AGO ARE NOW ACCEPTED AS FACT.

—Communications Intelligence
February 14, 2022

Critics are all failures. No one wants to be a critic. They're failed authors and screenwriters; they are dodgeball victims, and that's why these people are writing these little scathing reviews.

—Interview with *The Daily Show with Jon Stewart*
August 7, 2001

IF YOU'RE IN BUSINESS *and your business* **IS THE NEWS,** *and you want to* **GET MORE PEOPLE TO** *pay attention,* **YOU SHOULD BE HONEST.**

—*Interview with Fox News*
February 11, 2022

DISINFORMATION IS INDEED A GRAVE PROBLEM IN THE US. BUT IT LARGELY COMES FROM THE VERY CORPORATE MEDIA OUTLETS THAT MOST FLAMBOYANTLY CLAIM TO OPPOSE IT.

—GETTR
December 31, 2021

WHAT I'M WILLING TO DO IS LOOK STUPID.

—*The Joe Rogan Experience*
January 14, 2014

FREEDOM:

It's the most important
thing we have. It's what
makes this place special.
It's rare, and it's fragile.
Protect it at all costs.

—Instagram post
September 27, 2021

I TALK WILD.

—Interview with
Breaking Points
June 17, 2021

These are my
intentions and these
words broadcast my
feelings. If all of
a sudden you have
forbidden words that
doesn't make the
intent any better.
It's just appeasing
sensitive people.

—Interview with
Brightest Young Things
September 29, 2011

ONE OF THE REASONS

OUTRAGE AND FEAR

JOURNALISM IS SO
PROMINENT IS SIMPLY
BECAUSE WE FLOCK TO IT.

—Instagram post
September 26, 2021

GOVERNMENT
AND
POLITICS

" I WANT TO BE SOMEONE WHO CAN WATCH AND OBSERVE.

—The Joe Rogan Experience
March 19, 2022

"

FAITH ITSELF IS A HORRIBLE MECHANISM THAT STUNTS THE GROWTH OF IDEAS. IT ALSO STUNTS THE ACT OF QUESTIONING, AND IT DOES THIS BY PUSHING THE IDEA THAT YOU HAVE TO HAVE FAITH—AND THAT NOTHING HAS TO BE PROVEN.

—*Joe Rogan: Podcasts, Pot, and Persistence,*
by James Woolf, 2020

PEOPLE TREAT [POLITICS] LIKE SPORTS TEAMS. *"Democrats are pussies, man! The Republicans are going to kick their asses!"* . . . **THE GOVERNMENT'S HAPPY, BIG BUSINESS IS HAPPY,** *because either way they win.*

—Interview with the *Austin Chronicle*
   May 4, 2001

Human beings, for whatever reason, there's a percentage of us that lean towards conspiratorial thinking. THEY LEAN TOWARDS THINKING THAT THERE'S SOME SORT OF A PLOT AGAINST THEM, OR THE GOVERNMENT'S AGAINST THEM.

—*The Joe Rogan Experience*
March 15, 2020

When does a political ideology

BECOME A RELIGION?

When it comes to rely upon
easily debunked myths and
supernatural beliefs.

—*GETTR*
January 2, 2022

THE MORE REAL LIFE COMES INTO THE MEDIA, THE LESS POWER THE GOVERNMENT HAS OVER PEOPLE. ONCE THESE TABOOS ARE DROPPED, PEOPLE START QUESTIONING OTHER THINGS.

—Interview with the
Austin Chronicle
May 4, 2001

STAND-UP
COMEDY

IF YOU'RE NOT READY TO HAVE A GOOD TIME AND LISTEN TO WHAT I HAVE TO SAY, THEN I DON'T WANT YOU TO COME.

—Interview with the *Austin Chronicle*
May 4, 2001

THE COMICS I HATE
ARE THIEVES.
NOTHING'S MORE
DISGUSTING THAN
A GUY WHO STEALS
ANOTHER PERSON'S
IDEAS AND TRIES
TO CLAIM THEM
AS HIS OWN.

—*Joe Rogan: Podcasts,*
Pot, and Persistence,
by James Woolf, 2020

THE AUDIENCE CHANGES EVERY NIGHT. YOU'RE THE SAME PERSON. YOU HAVE TO SPEAK YOUR MIND AND DO THE STUFF THAT YOU THINK IS FUNNY AND MAKES YOU LAUGH.

—*Joe Rogan: Podcasts, Pot, and Persistence,*
  by James Woolf, 2020

I NEVER WANT TO COMPROMISE MY ACT JUST TO GET A LAUGH.

—IMDB

MY ACT IS SO
completely and totally
UNCENSORED
that the only way I could
REALLY PULL IT OFF
is if I treat the
AUDIENCE LIKE THEY'RE
my best friends.

—*Joe Rogan: A Biography*, by Nicholas Voth, 2020

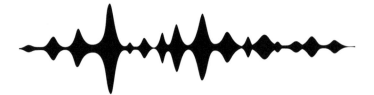

The misconception
is that stand-up
comics are always on.
I don't know any
really funny comics
that are annoying
and constantly
trying to be funny
all the time.

—*Joe Rogan: A Biography,*
by Nicholas Voth, 2020

TO ME, COMEDY IS A GREAT OCCUPATION BECAUSE I DON'T REALLY WORRY THAT MUCH ABOUT WHAT OTHER PEOPLE THINK OF ME.

—*Joe Rogan: A Biography,*
by Nicholas Voth, 2020

I have a big bond with strippers. The main thing is that we're both on the fringes of society. . . . [We] have a different way of looking at things.

—Interview with the *Austin Chronicle*
May 4, 2001

A comic's jokes, a comic's material, that's his thoughts, his view of the world, it's like a piece of your soul. Your thoughts on anything in life, whether it's racism or relationships or politics, whatever, that's *you.*

—Interview with the
Austin Chronicle
May 4, 2001

NOT ALL COMEDY CLUBS OR SITUATIONS ARE IDEAL, ESPECIALLY WHEN YOU'RE FIRST COMING UP, AND I THINK THAT'S GOOD FOR YOU. EVENTUALLY, YOU GET TO EXPRESS YOUR REAL PERSONALITY.

—*Joe Rogan: A Biography*, by Nicholas Voth, 2020

"

I'M REALLY HAPPY THAT I'VE BEEN ABLE TO MAKE PEOPLE LAUGH AND *distract them from their day-to-day bullshit at a* COMEDY SHOW OR BECAUSE THEY ENJOYED ONE OF MY CDS OR TV *specials, but I don't know how many people have* ACTUALLY HAD LIFE-CHANGING THOUGHTS BECAUSE OF IT.

—Reddit post
  November 20, 2014

One of the things that happened is I did a lot of shitty gigs. When you do a bunch of shitty bar gigs, YOU HAVE TO GET USED TO PEOPLE YELLING AT YOU, YOU'RE USED TO THINKING ON THE FLY, TO DEALING WITH WEIRD SITUATIONS.

—Interview with *Brightest Young Things*
October 16, 2014

PSYCHEDELICS AND OTHER **DRUGS**

REGULAR DMT
IS RICH WITH VISUALS.
VERY STRANGE,
BRIGHT, COLORFUL,
IMPOSSIBLE TO DESCRIBE
VISUALS.

—The Joe Rogan Experience
January 16, 2019

[With cannabis] I feel more vulnerable.

—*The Joe Rogan Experience*
January 16, 2019

IT'S A WEIRD EXPERIENCE
WHEN YOU'RE JUST TRYING
TO TALK OPENLY ABOUT HOW YOU
THINK PSYCHEDELIC DRUGS AND
MARIJUANA ARE BENEFICIAL. . . .
I FEEL LIKE YOU CAN LEARN
SOMETHING FROM THEM, FROM
MUSHROOMS, FROM PEYOTE,
FROM MARIJUANA. THEY
CAN BE USED AS A TOOL.

—Interview with *Brightest Young Things*
  September 29, 2011

[PSYCHEDELIC EXPERIENCES]

PUT IT ALL INTO PERSPECTIVE.
IT LETS YOU SEE THAT AS MUCH
AS THIS THING SEEMS TO BE
IMPORTANT, THIS IS ALL
TEMPORARY AND YOU'RE
A PART OF FOREVER.

—The Joe Rogan Experience
January 16, 2019

The number one reason why marijuana is illegal is because the Pharma Cartel does not want you to grow your own medicine. The Declaration of Independence was written on hemp paper. The first car ever made ran on hemp oil. Hemp seeds are also the healthiest food on the planet with the highest protein content out of any plant.

—*Joe Rogan: Podcasts, Pot, and Persistence,* by James Woolf, 2020

I definitely had one guy come up to me and ask if I knew where to get DMT. He had a crewcut and he didn't look like he'd ever done a drug in his life. He didn't seem curious; he seemed like he wanted to get me to do something. Like, you're the laziest narc ever, dude. This is ridiculous. What, do you think I bring drugs around with me?

—Interview with *Brightest Young Things,* September 29, 2011

"

I BROUGHT SOMETHING BACK FROM THOSE
EXPERIENCES [WITH DRUGS] WHICH MADE
ME SOFTER, OPEN TO OTHER IDEAS. . . .
BUT THERE'S ALWAYS SOME DUMB COP OUT
THERE WHO SAYS, "WE DON'T NEED ANOTHER
LEGAL DRUG AND THERE'S PSYCHOLOGICAL
ADDICTION AND BLAH BLAH BLAH."

—Interview with *Brightest Young Things*
September 29, 2011

"

MARIJUANA IS A TOOL TO HELP US.

YOU CAN ABUSE ANY TOOL THERE IS.

YOU CAN TAKE A HAMMER AND HIT YOURSELF IN THE HEAD IF YOU'RE STUPID.

YOU CAN ABUSE ANYTHING,

BUT YOU CAN ALSO USE IT AND BUILD YOURSELF A BEAUTIFUL HOUSE.

—*The Joe Rogan Experience*
January 16, 2019

PEOPLE DO ALWAYS TRY TO SMOKE POT WITH ME. BUT I THINK SOME OF THOSE PEOPLE ARE COPS.

—Interview with *Brightest Young Things*
September 29, 2011

[MARIJUANA] MAKES ME NICER. IT CALMS ME DOWN.

—*The Joe Rogan Experience*
January 16, 2019

[WITH DMT] YOU FEEL LIKE YOU'RE PART OF THE UNIVERSE. WHEN YOU'RE SEPARATE FROM YOUR EGO, YOU REALIZE YOU'RE A PART OF THIS WHOLE THING, AND THIS WHOLE THING IS UNSTOPPABLE.

—The Joe Rogan Experience
January 16, 2019

I HAVE MORE OF *a sense of* **COMMUNITY.** *I'm always* **HUGGING PEOPLE** *when I'm high.* **I WANT TO** *hug everybody.*

—*The Joe Rogan Experience*
January 16, 2019

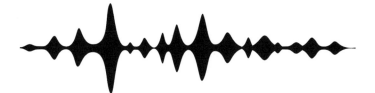

ON BEING
HAPPY

THE TIME YOU SPEND *hating on someone* **ROBS YOU OF** *your own time.* **YOU ARE LITERALLY** *hating on yourself* **AND YOU DON'T EVEN** *realize it.*

—*Joe Rogan: Podcasts, Pot, and Persistence,* by James Woolf, 2020

THE KEY TO
HAPPINESS DOESN'T
LAY IN NUMBERS IN
A BANK ACCOUNT
BUT IN THE WAY WE
MAKE OTHERS FEEL
AND THE WAY THEY
MAKE US FEEL.

—*Joe Rogan: Podcasts,
Pot, and Persistence,*
by James Woolf, 2020

I try to be
as nice as
possible to
everybody
I meet.

—Interview with *Huffington Post*
December 12, 2011

I REALIZED *a long time ago* **THAT INSTEAD OF** *being jealous you* **CAN BE INSPIRED** *and appreciative.* **IT CARRIES MORE** *energy to you.*

—Reddit post
November 20, 2014

I THINK A LOT
OF WHAT
HAPPINESS IS
IS A MANAGEMENT
ISSUE. ONE OF
THE BIG ONES
IS ELIMINATING
INTERACTIONS
WITH PEOPLE
THAT ARE
NEGATIVE.

—Youtube video
June 19, 2021

I THINK THE BEST
THING YOU CAN DO
IS CONSTANTLY
TRY TO IMPROVE
UPON YOUR WORK.
ALWAYS FOCUS ON THAT
FIRST AND FOREMOST.
[IF YOU CAN] EARNESTLY
TRY TO MAKE THINGS
THAT YOU REALLY ENJOY,
IT CAN ONLY BENEFIT
YOU IN THE LONG RUN.

—Reddit post
November 20, 2014

Live your life like there's a

DOCUMENTARY CREW

following you around and you
are analyzing your own behavior.
Do what you would want to do
so that your kids one day see
that documentary and look
on it with pride.

—YouTube video
March 3, 2018

WORK FOR THAT FEELING THAT YOU HAVE ACCOMPLISHED SOMETHING. DON'T WASTE YOUR TIME ON THIS EARTH WITHOUT MAKING A MARK.

—Joe Rogan: A Biography,
by Nicholas Voth, 2020

CAMARADERIE, LOVE, FAMILY, FRIENDSHIP, STRUGGLE, TESTING, LEARNING—ALL THOSE THINGS ARE IMPERATIVE. THEY'RE ALL A GIANT PART OF BEING A PERSON.

—Youtube video
June 19, 2021

We define ourselves far too often by our past failures. That's not you. You are this person right now. You're the person who has learned from those failures.

—*Joe Rogan: Podcasts, Pot, and Persistence,* by James Woolf, 2020

WHEN YOU'RE JEALOUS, ESPECIALLY OF SOMEONE ELSE'S ART OR CREATIONS, YOU AUTOMATICALLY PUT UP THESE SELFISH WALLS THAT REINFORCE YOUR STUPID IDEAS.

—Reddit post
November 20, 2014

THE RIGHT PATH TO
BEING A HAPPY,
HEALTHY PERSON IS
TO . . . TAKE CARE
OF YOUR BODY,
TAKE CARE OF
YOUR HEALTH,
TAKE CARE OF
YOUR MIND.

—YouTube video
November 7, 2017

THE MOST IMPORTANT
part of the
EQUATION IS
companionship,
FRIENDSHIP,
love, happiness,
SAFETY, SHELTER,
community.

—*Goalcast*
August 7, 2016

When you're around happy, inspirational people that are successful, it makes you feel better and you get inspired. And if you act on that inspiration, your life will be more fulfilled.

—YouTube video
June 19, 2021

CHOOSE
TO BE
INSPIRED.

—Reddit post
November 20, 2014

PEOPLE ARE FUEL.

When you meet these exceptional people that move you, what are the characteristics, what are the qualities that they have? [Let] those things become significant and important to you.

—YouTube video
June 19, 2021

YOU CAN, THROUGH A COMBINATION OF DISCIPLINE AND VISUALIZATION, CREATE A [SINGULAR] POSITIVITY IN YOUR LIFE . . . WHERE SUDDENLY, YOU DISCARD, LIKE A SNAKE SHEDDING ITS SKIN, YOU CAN LIKE DROP ALL THAT AND SUDDENLY EXPERIENCE SOME VERSION OF REBIRTH.

—*Goalcast*
   August 7, 2016

BE COOL TO PEOPLE.

BE NICE TO AS MANY PEOPLE AS YOU CAN. SMILE AT AS MANY PEOPLE AS YOU CAN. JUST DO THE MOST YOU CAN TO BE AS NICE AS YOU CAN.

—YouTube video
November 7, 2017

It's hard for people to be themselves. They don't like themselves. They don't like what they are, so they like to pretend there's something more exceptional. But what people really seem to enjoy is people . . . who just work at being a better person, being better at life.

—YouTube video
April 14, 2021

KINDNESS IS ONE OF *the best gifts* **YOU CAN BESTOW . . .** *We know that* **INHERENTLY THAT** *feels great.*

—*Joe Rogan: A Biography,*
by Nicholas Voth, 2020

"

If you live your life
JUST ACTING CONSTANTLY ON
THE MOMENTUM OF OTHER
people's expectations,
OR YOU WANTING TO BE LIKED
BY THESE OTHER PEOPLE,
you can run into a trap
AND SET YOURSELF UP FOR A LIFE
THAT YOU DIDN'T REALLY WANT.

—YouTube video
   November 7, 2017

Learn, learn, learn, ladies and gentlemen. I THINK IT'S VERY IMPORTANT TO CONTINUE TO CHALLENGE YOUR MIND.

—*The Atlantic*
August 19, 2019

What's interesting about science is that we're constantly discovering new things about the universe, about ourselves, about our bodies, about diseases, about the possibilities of the future. It's amazing. Science is one of the coolest things about being a human being—without a doubt.

—*Joe Rogan: A Biography,*
by Nicholas Voth, 2020

I think the best thing we can
do to change the world is to
INSPIRE YOUNG PEOPLE.
The more people realize
that the key to happiness in
life is to surround yourself
with good friends, to be a good
friend, to challenge yourself
in honest ways, to not take
shortcuts but rather to rise
to the challenge and grow
from the struggle.

—Caveman Circus
March 28, 2013

Mary Wood is a writer, political researcher, and mother of two curious boys. She lives in Northern New Jersey.